Alcohol

Alcohol

Elaine Landau

Franklin Watts
A Division of Scholastic Inc.
New York • Toronto • London • Auckland • Sydney
Mexico City • New Delhi • Hong Kong
Danbury, Connecticut

For Jason Garmizo

Note to readers: Definitions for words in **bold** can be found in the Glossary at the back of this book.

Photographs © 2003: Brown Brothers: 17; Corbis Images: 10 (Bettmann), 28 (Neal Preston), 6 (Nik Wheeler), 44 (Jenny Woodcock/Reflections Photolibrary); Fundamental Photos, New York/Richard Megna: cover; Getty Images/Liaison/Jim Bourg: 43; H. Armstrong Roberts, Inc./Charles Phelps Cushing: 19; ImageState/Cliff Hollenbeck: 8; North Wind Picture Archives: 14; Photo Researchers, NY: 5 left, 32 (Richard Hutchings), 27 (Dr. P. Marazzi/SPL); PhotoEdit: 46 (Mary Kate Denny), 2 (Tony Freeman), 35, 48 (Michael Newman), 9 (David Young-Wolff); Photri Inc./Dennis MacDonald: 5 right, 23; Stock Boston/Bob Daemmrich: 38; Stock Montage, Inc.: 16; Stone/Getty Images: 40 (Frank Siteman), 50 (David Young-Wolff); The Image Works: 30 (Bob Daemmrich), 20 (Larry Mulvehill); TimePix/Marc Asnin: 24.

The photograph on the cover shows a glass and a pitcher containing beer. The photograph opposite the title page shows two young people talking at a party.

Library of Congress Cataloging-in-Publication Data

Landau, Elaine.
    Alcohol / by Elaine Landau
       p. cm. — (Watts library)
    Includes bibliographical references and index.
    Summary: Discusses the health issues associated with alcohol, the history of alcohol use in the United States, and treatment options for those with an addiction to alcohol.
     ISBN 0-531-12023-6 (lib. bdg.)   0-516-16665-1 (pbk.)
    1. Alcoholism—United States—Juvenile literature. [1. Alcoholism.] I. Title. II. Series.
HV5066 .L423 2003
613.81—dc21   2001008405

Contents

A waitress serves a customer a drink at a restaurant, one of the many places people consume alcohol.

Chapter One

Alcohol

Alcohol is all around us. Countless bars and liquor stores dot America's landscape. Fine restaurants serve fine wines. An array of other alcoholic beverages are also available.

Turn on the TV—before long there will be a beer commercial. Beer and liquor ads peer out at us from the pages of magazines as well. These ads show beautiful people in glamorous situations. All are drinking and smiling.

Undoubtedly, alcohol is part of America's culture. At weddings we toast the bride and groom. Ships are blessed by

At many weddings, it is traditional to toast the bride and groom with champagne.

breaking a bottle of champagne. Wine is sometimes used in religious rites and ceremonies.

Alcohol is often a big part of holiday celebrations. Christmas cheer does not only mean yuletide jokes. There's alcohol in the eggnog. Beer can frequently be found at Fourth of July picnics. Perhaps the holiday most commonly associated with alcohol is New Year's Eve. Traditionally the new year is welcomed with a toast. Usually there's also drinking throughout the evening.

How Much Is Too Much?

You may have heard a lot about alcohol. People have many different ideas about this exceedingly popular substance. Some think that drinking alcohol is always harmful. They believe that even though adults are legally allowed to drink, they should not. Others hold the opposite view. They feel that

8

there is absolutely nothing wrong with adults drinking whenever they wish.

Yet neither of these notions is on target. According to the National Institute on Alcohol Abuse and Alcoholism, adults can regularly consume a moderate amount of alcohol safely. Doing so can even help prevent certain types of heart disease.

What is a moderate amount? For an adult female or someone over 65 years of age, moderate means just one drink. For a male, moderate drinking means two drinks.

Two-thirds of adults in the United States consume alcoholic beverages from time to time. Most people who drink do so responsibly. Nevertheless, a small percentage of people drink heavily. In these cases the end result can be devastating. Too much alcohol does serious harm to the body. It can also have a negative impact on relationships with family members and friends. People who drink excessively often experience difficulties at work as well. Though it is illegal, some young people also drink. The average age at which a group of 12- to 17-year-olds claimed to have had their first drink was at 12 years, 8 months old.

What Is a Drink?

A standard drink is
- One 12-ounce bottle of beer or wine cooler
- One 5-ounce glass of wine
- One and a half ounces of 80-proof distilled spirits

Each of these is equal in alcohol content to the others. They are each one drink.

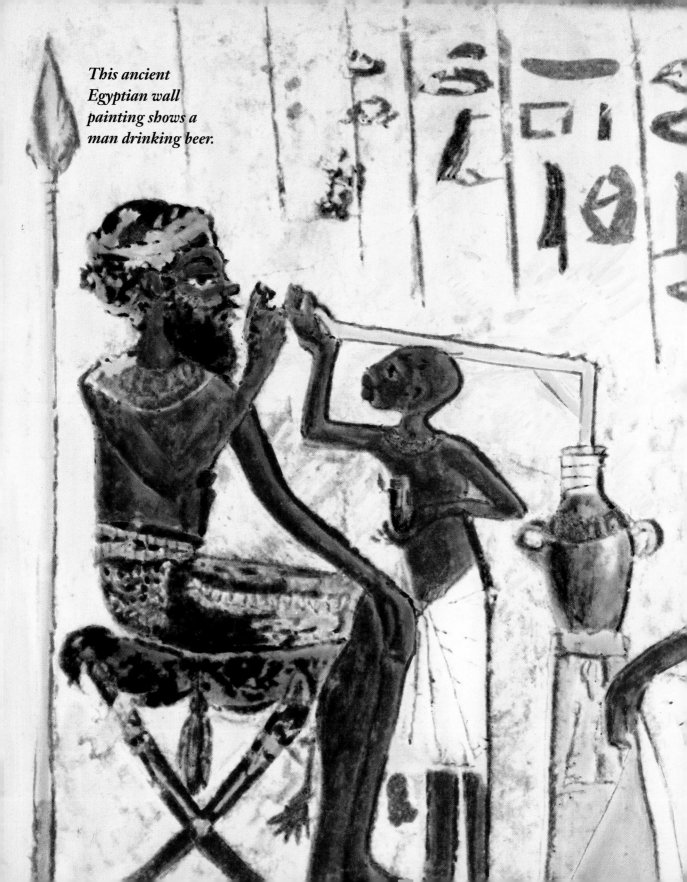

This ancient Egyptian wall painting shows a man drinking beer.

Chapter Two

Alcohol Through the Ages

If you think people only began drinking alcohol in modern times—think again. The practice dates back thousands of years. Wall paintings uncovered in ancient Egyptian tombs reveal that alcohol consumption was common there. Among the ancient Egyptians' favorite alcoholic beverages was a brew known as red beer. The key ingredients in it were under-baked bread, water, and crushed wheat.

Anthropologists, individuals who study how people live, suggest that the practice was widespread. They believe that ancient people readily discovered that alcohol could be produced from any fermentable material. When substances **ferment**, a chemical change takes place, causing the sugar in them to turn to alcohol.

In many parts of the world, berries and fruits were used for this purpose. In the tropics, sap taken from palm trees was made into alcohol. In central Asia people often drank **koumiss**. Koumiss was made from fermented mare's or camel's milk. Honey and water were used to make an alcoholic beverage known as **mead**. Mead was especially popular in northern Europe.

A Choice in the Colonies

Alcohol has been popular in the United States since colonial times. Instead of water, the Pilgrims brought barrels of beer with them aboard the *Mayflower*. This was a common practice in the days before refrigeration.

There wasn't any pumpkin pie at the first Thanksgiving, since the settlers had used up their supply of flour. However, beer, brandy, gin, and wine were not in short supply for the event. The colonists also made alcoholic beverages out of the vegetables they grew. These included beets, squash, corn, carrots, and tomatoes.

Alcohol in the Morning

Beer and sharp cider—alcoholic apple cider—largely replaced water as a typical drink in the colonies. These beverages were considered freer of impurities and therefore safer to drink. Having a mug of beer or sharp cider each morning was a common practice in many colonial homes. John Adams, our second president, claimed that starting the day with sharp cider calmed his stomach. Such beverages were even given to children!

Nevertheless, the early settlers did not walk around in a drunken stupor. It was realized that excessive drinking could hurt the colonies' well being. Alcohol may have been legal, but early on, there were attempts to control its use. This was a trend that would continue in the years ahead. Alcohol would be part of everyday life for many people. Yet at the same time, there would be restrictions regarding the use of alcohol.

At the very least, colonists were fined for drunken behavior. Depending on the colony and the particular law, drunkenness could also be punished with flogging—being beaten with a whip or a stick—or imprisonment. In addition, persons operating taverns needed licenses to do so. Fines were imposed for selling alcohol to someone who was already **intoxicated**. In many colonies individuals could be fined for selling alcohol to American Indians as well.

However, colonists depended on alcohol for more than their drinking pleasure. It proved to be a financial boon for some. Manufacturing rum was an extremely profitable industry in colonial New England. Tavern owners were often

Brewers as Community Pillars

William Penn, the founder of the Pennsylvania colony, began the colony's first brewery in 1638.

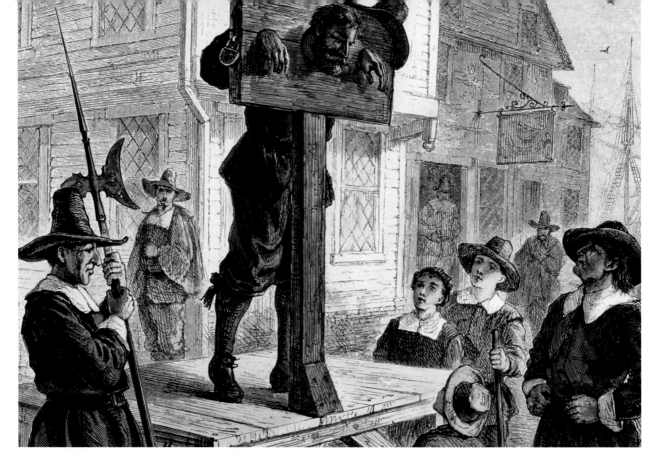

In colonial times, people who drank too much were often punished.

highly regarded and among the wealthiest members of the community.

Taverns were frequently more than just drinking establishments. Sometimes court was held there. Until churches were built, religious services were often conducted in taverns.

The Whiskey Rebellion

The early settlers' belief that they had a right to distill and drink alcohol spread westward as the country grew. This was evident in 1794, when distillers in western Pennsylvania tried to resist a government tax on whiskey. The rebellion failed, but it served as a protest. Americans felt they should not be taxed for what they saw as a basic right—that of brewing and drinking alcohol.

Alcohol as a Dangerous Influence

Yet toward the end of the 1700s some people began to question the place of alcohol in everyday life. Antialcohol groups, known as **temperance societies**, started to take root. They regarded alcohol as a dangerous influence and argued that it led to immoral behavior. These groups claimed that alcohol made men miss work and church services, as well as stray from their wives.

Temperance societies actively campaigned against alcohol and over time drew others to their cause. In the 1840s and 1850s a number of states passed **prohibition** laws banning the use of alcohol. These laws did not last very long. They were eventually vetoed by governors or repealed by state legislatures. A few laws were declared invalid by state supreme courts.

Nevertheless, temperance crusaders refused to give up. In 1874 the Women's Christian Temperance Union (WCTU) was born. This group launched a remarkably effective campaign against alcohol. People were asked to sign **abstinence** pledges. Schoolchildren were taught songs praising **sobriety**. They were given children's readers on the dangers of entering a saloon.

Temperance policy became a part of public education. The goal was to stop young people before they went astray. By 1902 temperance education was part of the public school curriculum in every state but Arizona.

As fervor for temperance spread, politicians began to champion the cause. By 1913 a number of states had once

COLD WATER ARMY PLEDGE.

We, Cold Water Girls and Boys,[a] | Wine, Beer, and Cider we detest,[d]
Freely renounce the treacherous joys[b] | And thus we'll make our parents blest ;[e]
Of Brandy, Whiskey, Rum, and Gin ; | "So here we pledge[f] perpetual hate[g]
The Serpent's lure to death and sin :[c] | To all that can Intoxicate."[h]

a Prov. viii. 4: Zech. viii. 5.   b Isa. lvi. 12; v. 11, 12: xxviii. 7: Prov. xx. 1.   c Prov. xxiii. 32: I. Peter v. 8.   d Eph. v. 18: Prov. xxiii. 31: Deut. vii. 26.   e Prov. x. 1: xxiii. 15: III. John 4.   f Jer. xxxv. 6.   g Ps. xcvii. 10: Rom. xii. 9: Ps. cxix. 128.   h Rom. xiv. 21.

CERTIFICATE OF MEMBERSHIP.

This Certifies, That *Isabella F Hamilton* having taken the above Pledge, is a Member of the **CONNECTICUT COLD WATER ARMY.**

Countersigned,   *Th. S. Williams* President Conn. Temp. Society.

Olcott Allen
Leader of the   Division.   *Chas J Warren* Secretary.

again passed prohibition laws. In nine states alcohol was outlawed statewide. In others individual towns were given the option of banning alcoholic beverages by local **ordinance**. Through these measures nearly half of all Americans now lived with prohibition.

Carrie Nation

Among the most colorful members of the Women's Christian Temperance Union was a woman from Kansas named Carrie Nation. Standing nearly 6 feet (1.85 meters) tall and weighing more than 180 pounds (82 kilograms), Nation cut quite an imposing figure. Her zeal for temperance had been fueled by a brief marriage to a heavy drinker, and she proved to be a fierce foe of whiskey brewers and saloon keepers.

Armed with a Bible in one hand and a hatchet in the other, Nation led her followers in destroying one saloon after another. Her battle cry was "Smash, ladies, smash!" As liquor bottles and glasses flew off shelves, the women managed to at least temporarily shut down a

number of drinking establishments. Between 1900 and 1910, Carrie Nation was arrested some thirty times for her actions, but that did not stop her. She felt that she answered to a higher calling.

Temperance supporters wanted more though. They had dreamed of an alcohol-free, or **dry**, country. In January 1919, their dream came true. The Eighteenth Amendment to the Constitution was ratified. This amendment ushered in Prohibition on a national scale. It made alcohol an illegal substance throughout the United States.

Prohibition

Prohibition became the law of the land—yet it eventually failed. There had been some early warning signs. Three months before the amendment was passed, more than half a million dollars worth of liquor was stolen from government warehouses.

Despite Prohibition, alcohol remained accessible. The new law opened the door to the **bootleg** trade. Illegal distilleries and **stills** sprang up in many parts of the United States. Instead of going to bars and saloons, some people now frequented **speakeasies**, which were illegal drinking establishments.

Smuggling thrived during Prohibition as well. Ships known as rumrunners brought in alcoholic beverages from Belgium, Holland, and other nations. Between 1923 and 1925, 370 such vessels were seized. A great deal of alcohol was also smuggled across the Canadian border. All together, it is estimated that nearly $40 million worth of alcohol was illegally brought into the United States each year.

Prohibition also kept the courts and law enforcement agencies busy. Early on, courts became bogged down with pending liquor violation cases. In just the first three years of Prohibition, thirty Prohibition enforcement agents were killed on the job. Convictions for alcohol-related crimes nearly doubled as well.

Interestingly, an increased number of younger people began drinking during the early years of Prohibition. Between 1919 and 1926, eight state mental hospitals reported that

Speakeasies

During the time of prohibition, it has been estimated that there were as many as 500,000 speakeasies in operation.

more teenage patients were admitted for alcohol-related problems than in the past. Many of these individuals had been high school students. Prohibition was supposed to protect young people from alcohol, but it had actually spurred them on to drink.

It was clear that prohibition wasn't working. Some felt that drinking alcohol was too much a part of American culture to put a halt to it. Before long the social and political tide openly turned against Prohibition. On December 5, 1933, Congress adopted the Twenty-First Amendment to the Constitution. This effectively repealed the Eighteenth Amendment. Prohibition had lasted thirteen years. Now it was over. Americans were again legally free to drink alcohol.

Prohibition officers capture a ship containing hundreds of cases of champagne, beer, and liquor.

People crowd a German beer hall to celebrate Octoberfest.

Chapter Three

Physical Effects of Alcohol

Today, alcohol remains extremely popular. More people around the globe use alcohol than any other stimulant or depressant with the exception of caffeine. Alcohol is not digested like a food. Instead it is quickly absorbed into the bloodstream through the stomach and gastrointestinal tract.

How quickly someone becomes intoxicated—or drunk— depends on a number of different factors. The kind and amount of alcohol consumed has a bearing, as does the quantity of food eaten beforehand. Other factors include how quickly the alcohol was ingested as well as the drinker's weight, age, mood, health, and prior drinking habits.

People often say that they get "high" from alcohol. However, alcohol is actually a depressant. It depresses the central nervous system. That means that the person's breathing and heart rate are slowed. Alcohol also hinders a person's reaction time, coordination, and judgment.

The end result is that someone who has been drinking is less able to perform complex tasks. Driving a car or operating heavy machinery can be hazardous. It doesn't matter whether that individual has done these things for years while sober. Alcohol completely changes a person's ability to function.

Blood Alcohol Concentration (BAC)

You can find out how intoxicated someone is by determining the level of alcohol in his or her blood. That percentage is known as the person's **blood alcohol concentration** (BAC). In many states a BAC of 0.08 to 0.10 percent is the legal limit set for driving a vehicle. Anyone driving with a higher BAC can be arrested for driving while intoxicated (DWI).

Yet a person's ability to safely drive actually decreases at a much lower BAC. With a BAC of just 0.02 percent, a driver will have difficulty steering a car while reacting to ordinary changes in traffic. Drinking and driving can be devastating. Every 32 minutes someone dies in an alcohol-related traffic incident. It has been further shown that about two out of every five Americans will be in a car crash in which alcohol is a factor.

A drunk driver had a disastrous

A police officer uses a device to determine whether this driver is intoxicated.

effect on the lives of Giovanni Vaccarello and his family. One night the Vaccarellos were leaving a catering hall when a drunk driver came barreling down the street at 70 miles (112 km) per hour. It was after dark, but the car's headlights were not on. They never saw him coming as they crossed the street. After the driver ran a red light, he slammed into the family.

Giovanni and his daughter were hurled into the air. His daughter clung to life for a few hours before dying. His other daughter went through the windshield and was carried 150 feet (45.7 m). She died instantly. So did Giovanni's wife, who was dragged 180 feet (54.8 m) by the car. Besides suffering a heart attack, Giovanni's left leg was broken in

Giovanni Vaccarello stands with his son outside the courthouse during the trial of the drunk driver that killed three members of his family.

three places. "If he came at me with a gun, I've got a chance," the injured man said of the drunk driver. "But not with a five-ton car."

Side Effects of Alcohol

Alcohol also negatively interacts with more than 150 different medications. Some of these are prescription drugs, but others are over-the-counter medicines purchased by people every day. Antibiotics are frequently prescribed to fight infections, but alcohol reduces their effectiveness. Someone taking tranquilizers for stress or antihistamines for a cold or allergy may experience some drowsiness. However, if he or she drinks even a small amount of alcohol, this effect can be greatly enhanced. Under these circumstances, the person's ability to concentrate is lessened. Operating certain types of machinery can become dangerous.

Alcohol can also affect a pregnant woman's unborn baby. It is now known that alcohol can cause a wide range of birth

Alcohol and Accidents

According to the Centers for Disease Control (CDC), each year about 30,000 deaths resulting from both recreational and on-the-job accidents are linked to alcohol.

defects. Among the most serious of these is fetal alcohol syndrome (FAS). FAS is an irreversible condition. There is no cure for it. Children born with FAS may have heart defects or other physical abnormalities, such as having an unusually small head and upper jaw. Often there are serious learning disabilities as well. In some cases lifelong behavior problems can occur.

Presently scientists are not certain of the amount of alcohol that causes birth defects. The best way to prevent alcohol-related birth defects for pregnant women, or any woman trying to become pregnant, is not to drink at all.

Too Much Alcohol Takes Its Toll

Heavy drinking over a long period of time can result in a number of serious health problems. Prolonged and excessive use of alcohol can lead to heart disease. It also increases the risk for high blood pressure and stroke. Over time, alcohol can also have destructive effects on many of the body's organs, such as the liver and the pancreas.

Excessive long-term alcohol use can play havoc with the drinker's liver. One consequence can be alcoholic hepatitis. This is actually an inflammation of the liver. It causes intense abdominal pain. The person also experiences jaundice, which is a yellowing of the skin, eyeballs, and urine. If the individual continues drinking, alcoholic hepatitis can result in death. However, if he or she is able to permanently stop, the condition can sometimes be reversed.

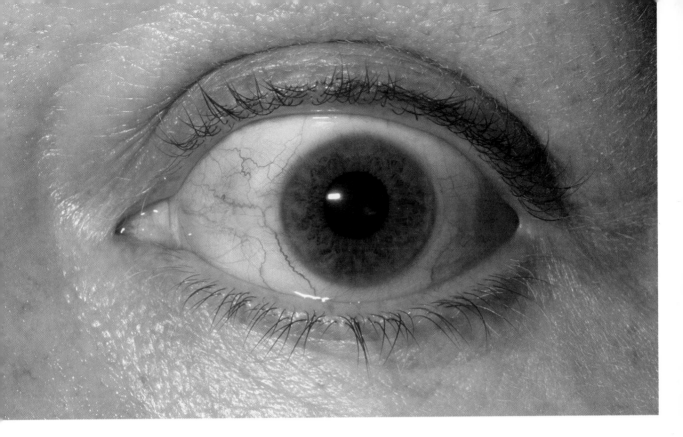

Another serious alcohol-related liver disease is alcoholic cirrhosis, or scarring of the liver. Between 10 and 20 percent of heavy drinkers eventually develop this condition. Unlike alcoholic hepatitis, alcoholic cirrhosis cannot be reversed. If the person does not stop drinking, it can be fatal. In severe cases a liver transplant may be necessary.

One well-known person who had a liver transplant because of alcohol abuse is rock musician David Crosby. By the time he reached his fifties, Crosby seemed to be doing well. His music was well received, and he had stopped abusing both alcohol and drugs. Yet the effect of years of hard drinking on his body could not be easily wiped away. He described what happened this way:

Yellowing of the skin and eyes is one way to tell if someone has jaundice.

"When I started having severe stomachaches and bloating and tightness in my abdomen, I ignored it. But by June the pains were so bad that several times I had to be helped back to the bus after the show, and . . . I had to miss a performance in Salt Lake City."

After an examination and a series of tests, doctors discovered that Crosby's liver had deteriorated. Without a transplant, they felt, he had about six months left to live. Fortunately, four months after his diagnosis, an organ became available and Crosby underwent a successful transplant.

"I know some people think I got special treatment because I was a celebrity—especially since the average wait is six months to a year—and I didn't deserve a transplant after my years of drug [and alcohol] use," Crosby noted. "But the people who assign the organs didn't care who I was—their determining factors are proximity to the organ, blood type, body

Musician David Crosby nearly died because of his substance abuse problems. Crosby needed to take medication to help his body accept his new liver.

Heart Smart Drinking

Unlike heavy drinking, moderate drinking can have a beneficial effect on the heart. This is especially true for those at greatest risk for heart attacks—men over 45 years of age and women over 50. A new study seems to suggest that even people who have had heart attacks do not always have to stop drinking. Drinking moderately may reduce the chances of a second heart attack.

size, and your medical condition. And my history didn't matter, because the doctor's primary considerations are, will this person die without it and will this person do everything to make it work. In my case, since I had stopped doing drugs [and alcohol], the answer to both was yes."

Besides the liver, alcohol can also damage the pancreas. The pancreas is an important organ. It plays a role in digestion and how the nutrients we eat are used by the body. It also helps to control our blood sugar levels by producing a hormone known as insulin. Heavy drinking for a long period of time can cause the pancreas to become inflamed. This condition is called pancreatitis. Pancreatitis results in both severe abdominal pain and weight loss. In some cases it is fatal.

Drinking heavily for years on end can also increase a person's risk for certain types of cancer. These include cancer of the mouth, throat, larynx, and esophagus. Further data suggest that using alcohol excessively also heightens the risk of developing colon and rectal cancer. Women having two or more drinks a day are at slightly higher risk for breast cancer as well.

From work or school to home, heavy drinking can affect every aspect of a person's life.

Chapter Four

Alcoholism and Alcohol Abuse

Many people know that heavy drinking can have a devastating effect on both their health and personal lives. People who drink excessively tend to experience problems with family members, coworkers, and friends. They often find it difficult to meet deadlines and frequently become less productive. At times they lose their jobs, worsening their problems.

Almost one in five adult Americans lived with an alcoholic while growing up.

The children of heavy drinkers are often severely affected by their parents' problem. In one case, both parents of a young boy had tried to stop drinking twice, but his father had a relapse. His mother also suffered from depression. He described what things were like for him growing up, as follows:

"That could be pretty disruptive to a household, scary. She'd [his mother] get weird. We'd be out on a vacation, and she would be silent and moody, and obviously in a space where we couldn't ever really reach her—just be real weepy. And so we'd be out on this vacation, and we'd have to go home all of a sudden. [I was] thirteen, fourteen when I realized this was going on. And I blamed myself."

Later on, the boy began drinking heavily himself. He further described how he felt then: "There was a period of time when I just didn't care if I died or not. I would go out and drink [and] got in a legal scrape or two."

Despite the detrimental effects of alcohol, in many cases heavy drinkers seem unable to stop or to even reduce their alcohol intake. Ten percent of elementary schoolchildren report that they have had alcohol. By the time they are high school students, 3.4 percent report that they drink daily. It has also been estimated that almost 14 million Americans, or one out of every thirteen people, regularly drink to excess. Millions more drink more than they should at times. More than half of all Americans claim that at least one of their close relatives has a drinking problem.

Danger Ahead!

Studies show that people who drink too much are more likely to commit a violent crime or become a victim of violence.

Symptoms of Alcoholism

Frequently heavy drinkers are suffering from a disease known as alcoholism. This illness is characterized by the following:

- *Craving.* An alcoholic experiences an overwhelming urge to drink. The feeling often overpowers his or her better judgment. Some claim that it "owns their soul."

- *Loss of control.* Once an alcoholic has begun to drink, that individual may feel unable to stop.

- *Physical dependence.* The alcoholic's body becomes used to alcohol. A physical reaction results when he or she stops drinking. There may be nausea, sweating, shaking, and feelings of anxiety. These are known as withdrawal symptoms.

- *Tolerance.* Over time an alcoholic needs more alcohol than before to experience feeling intoxicated, a "high," from it.

When dealing with alcoholism, it is not a question of what the person drinks or how long he or she has been drinking. The problem is that the alcoholic is gripped by an overwhelming need for alcohol. Some may say that these individuals should exercise more self-control, but it is extremely difficult for most alcoholics to stop drinking without help. Alcohol is a drug. Some people become addicted to it, just as they might to an illegal drug.

Newspaper columnist Pete Hamill knew the feeling well. In his book *A Drinker's Life*, he described what it was like: "If I wrote a good column for the newspaper, I'd go to the bar and celebrate; if I wrote a poor column, I would drink away my

regret. Then I'd go home, another dinner missed, another chance to play with the children gone, and in the morning, hungover, thick-tongued, and thick-fingered, I'd attempt through my disgust to make amends."

Young people can experience similar feelings. This is how it was for Norm who discovered beer when he was thirteen. "I drank every chance I got and liked everything about it—the way that beer tasted and especially the way it made me feel. . ." Norm recalled. "It's funny, the way I changed so fast.

For many young people, alcohol can become an addiction.

When I was twelve years old, I thought I'd be a cop or a teacher when I got older. One year later, all I could think about was getting older so I could buy as much beer as I wanted, with no questions asked. Because I was hung over and shaky every morning, I started having trouble in school. I couldn't keep my mind on anything. I couldn't even write down my homework assignments, much less do them."

Alcoholism— Genes or Environment?

It is often asked why some people can drink without becoming alcoholics and others cannot. Alcoholism sometimes seems to run in families. However, scientists are not sure whether this is due to genes, environment, or a combination of both. The most recent research suggests that several genes are involved in predisposing someone to alcoholism. Each of these may be partly responsible for placing a person at risk for the disease.

Yet while genes play a role in this illness, other factors do too. Some of these are psychological. Many people drink to block out emotional pain. People who feel they don't quite measure up may be more likely to turn to alcohol. Impulsiveness—the tendency to act on sudden urges—has been linked to alcohol use as well.

In addition, social factors weigh in. Someone whose friends and family don't drink may be less likely to start drinking. The availability of alcohol is still another piece of this puzzle.

Alcohol Abuse

Not everyone who drinks too much, or sometimes drinks when they should not, is an alcoholic. Many people simply abuse alcohol. Unlike alcoholics, alcohol abusers usually do not become physically dependent on alcohol. Nevertheless, at times they drink to excess with devastating consequences.

According to the National Institute on Alcohol Abuse and Alcoholism (NIAAA), a person is abusing alcohol if one or more of the following situations repeatedly occur within a one-year period:

- Failing to fulfill major work, home, or school responsibilities, such as missing too many days of work or consistently failing to turn in homework.
- Drinking in situations that are physically dangerous, such as before driving a car or operating machinery.
- Having school-related legal problems, such as destroying school property or physically hurting someone while drunk.

Children of alcoholics are more likely to become alcoholics than children of non-alcoholic parents.

- Continued drinking despite having ongoing relationship problems that are caused or worsened by the effects of alcohol.

Not everyone who has an alcohol problem knows it, even though it may be obvious to those around that person. Yet 8 million Americans suffer from alcoholism, while another 6 million abuse alcohol. The children of alcoholics are two to seven times more likely than the general population to experience problems with alcohol later in life.

Alcohol can ruin a young person's health and mental well-being.

Chapter Five

Alcohol and Youth

Alcohol is just as big a problem for many young people as it is for many adults. Though young people are not legally allowed to drink, there are still substantial numbers of underage drinkers. In fact, underage drinking has been identified as the nation's number one drug problem. Young people who chose to drink frequently experience problems with their schoolwork, friends, and parents.

The National Institute on Alcohol Abuse and Alcoholism released these little known, but alarming, facts surrounding drinking and young people:

- Forty percent of children who begin drinking before the age of fifteen will become alcoholics sometime in their lives.
- Twenty-four percent of eighth graders have used alcohol in the last thirty days.
- Ninth graders who drink are almost twice as likely to attempt suicide as those who don't.
- Three million children ages fourteen through seventeen are regular drinkers who already have a confirmed alcohol problem.

Effects on the Brain

There is growing evidence that even a single drink can impair learning and memory in young people. In memory tests taken after the equivalent of two drinks, younger subjects performed significantly worse than older ones. The memory loss lasts as long as the young person is under the influence of alcohol.

The situation is worse for children and teens who drink significant amounts over an extended period. New studies suggest that heavy alcohol use can impair brain function in adolescents. At this time scientists do not know whether this damage can be reversed.

Serious Consequences

Sometimes consequences of drinking are much more immediate. Binge drinking and drinking contests have occurred at parties among both high school and college students. At these events, some students may try to see who can drink the most in the least amount of time. However, drinking too much too fast puts people at risk for alcohol poisoning, which can be fatal.

A University of Michigan study revealed that 15 percent of eighth graders, 25 percent of tenth graders, and 31 percent of twelfth graders had engaged in binge drinking. Binge drinking for males is defined as having at least five drinks in a row. For females, it's four drinks.

Binge drinking was fatal for Scott S. Krueger, a college freshman at Massachusetts Institute of Technology (MIT) in Boston. Krueger was found unconscious in his room after he had been drinking with his friends at a fraternity event. The young man was rushed to the hospital, where it was learned that his blood alcohol concentration was 0.41 percent. This meant that he had swallowed at least sixteen drinks. There was only about a 50 percent chance that he would survive. Sadly, he did not. Scott Krueger remained in a coma for three days before dying.

One night of drinking led to Scott S. Krueger's death.

His death is not an isolated case. Similar incidents have occurred elsewhere. Alcohol has often had a devastating effect on the lives of young people. Some have died due to alcohol poisoning. Other times intoxicated young people have drowned or been killed in sports-related or driving accidents.

While asking for help can be difficult, it is the first step in solving your drinking problem.

Chapter Six

Treatment and Change

Admitting that help is needed for an alcohol problem is frequently not easy. This is especially true for young people. Often they think of people with alcohol problems as being old or living on the street. In our society excessive drinking is sometimes viewed as a sign of weakness. However, alcoholism is a disease and should be looked at as such. Someone struggling with alcoholism is not any weaker than a person trying to control diabetes or asthma.

Young people who think that they may have a drinking problem should find a responsible adult to talk to. The person can be a guidance counselor, teacher, or relative. This can be a first step toward getting help. Someone who feels uncomfortable approaching a person he or she knows should try calling an alcohol or drug abuse hotline instead. Your local library can provide the most current hotline numbers.

Treatment and Young People

Helping children and teens with alcohol problems differs somewhat from treating adults. Professionals working with

Young people at a treatment facility discuss their problems with alcohol.

young people remain mindful of the youth's age and abilities. Certain factors that often affect preteens and teens are taken into consideration too, such as the influence of friends and school-related pressures.

Treating young people involves working with their families as well. This is especially important because sometimes the young person's family is a factor in the problem. The child or adolescent will have to live and deal with their family for quite some time.

There are a number of different treatment choices. The type of treatment chosen may depend on how severe the young person's problem is. Teens with serious drinking problems may enter a residential treatment program. They live at a center while being helped. Depending on their progress, they may remain there from about one month to a year.

In some cases the first phase of treatment is **detoxification**. This involves purging the person's system of alcohol. After that, the young person begins to learn to lead a healthier existence. These treatment centers were first developed for adults. However, many have now adjusted their programs to meet the needs of adolescents with the severest alcohol abuse problems.

A young person and his mother meet with a counselor to talk about issues related to his alcoholism.

Some young drinkers find help through various counseling programs. Individuals involved in these programs live at home. The counseling sessions help them to recognize the feelings that trigger their need for alcohol and better deal with these emotions. The young patient's family takes part in the program as well.

Numerous young people with alcohol problems also attend

Alcoholics Anonymous (AA) meetings. Alcoholics Anonymous is a fellowship made up of more than 2 million recovered alcoholics in the United States and other nations. At meetings people share their experiences. They offer support as they "help each other to stay sober."

Prevention

Some people believe that prevention is as important as cure. They feel that alcohol is too highly valued in our society and want to turn things around. Many people are taking steps in that direction.

Numerous community centers now hold monthly alcohol-free parties for those under twenty-one. Towns offer alcohol-free family New Year's Eve events as well. Often junior high and high schools provide resistance skills training. This training gives young people the necessary social skills to resist alcohol. Many youths have signed pledges not to drink and drive or accept a ride from someone who has been drinking. Others have pledged not to drink until they are twenty-one.

Students are doing even more. In the fall of 2000, 435 high school students—one from each congressional district in the country—went to Washington, D.C. They met with lawmakers, celebrities, and medical professionals to discuss the problem of underage drinking. By the time they left, the teens had come up with a list of recommended policy changes. They presented these at a national news conference on Capitol Hill.

Many young people are learning to say no when pressured by friends to drink.

Often attitude changes begin on a smaller scale. It may start with a single person speaking his or her mind. That happened in Lemont, Illinois, when a fourteen-year-old softball player named Krystle Newquist refused to wear her team's jersey. The team's sponsor was a local tavern, and its name was clearly printed across the shirt. "I hate alcohol," Krystle explained. "And if I put the uniform on, I would be a walking billboard for it."

Local league officials refused to let the girl play unless she wore the jersey. Krystle never gave in and sat out the rest of the season. Krystle's grandfather had died due to alcoholism, and she did not want to encourage anyone to drink.

Krystle Newquist put her values above playing a sport she loved. "I will only play softball for three or four more years," she noted. "But everything I stand for will be with me for the rest of my life." Other people have taken similar stands. Sometimes change comes slowly—one step at a time.

Dying for a Drink

One hundred thousand Americans die from alcohol-related causes each year.

Timeline

1770s	The colonists in early America enjoy alcoholic beverages.
1794	Whiskey distillers protest a tax on alcohol in western Pennsylvania. This event becomes known as the Whiskey Rebellion.
1840s–50s	The temperance movement begins to take root.
1874	The Women's Christian Temperance Union is established. It proves to be an effective force for banning alcohol.
1919	The Eighteenth Amendment to the Constitution is ratified, making alcohol illegal in the United States.
1933	The Twenty-First Amendment to the Constitution is passed, repealing the Eighteenth Amendment. Alcohol is once again legal.
1935	Alcoholics Anonymous is founded.
1966	Alcoholism is recognized as a medical illness by the American Medical Association.
1974	The National Institute on Alcohol Abuse and Alcoholism (NIAAA) is established.
1994	The drug naltrexone is approved for the treatment of alcohol.
1997	A Harvard School of Public Health study reveals that large numbers of junior high and high school students engage in binge drinking.
2000	A published NIAAA study indicates that heavy alcohol use can impair brain function in adolescents.

Glossary

abstinence—the practice of not drinking alcohol

alcoholism—a disease in which a person becomes physically addicted to alcohol

anthropologist—a person who studies how people live

blood alcohol concentration—the level of alcohol in a person's blood

bootleg—to illegally smuggle liquor

detoxification—the process of purging a person's system of alcohol

dry—without alcohol

ferment—a chemical process through which the sugar in a substance turns to alcohol

intoxicated—the state of having had too much alcohol or being "drunk"

koumiss—an alcoholic beverage made from fermented mare's or camel's milk

mead—an alcoholic beverage made from honey and water

ordinance—a decree or ruling

prohibition—the act of outlawing the use of alcohol

sobriety—the state of being alcohol-free

speakeasy—an illegal drinking establishment

still—a mechanism used to make alcoholic beverages

temperance society—a group opposed to the use of alcohol

To Find out More

Books

Aaseng, Nathan. *Teens and Drunk Driving*. San Diego: Lucent Books, 2000.

Claypool, Jane. *Alcohol and You*. Danbury, CT: Franklin Watts, 1997.

Clayton, Lawrence. *Alcohol*. Berkeley Heights, NJ: Enslow Publishers, 1999.

Haughton, Emma. *Alcohol*. Austin, TX: Raintree/Steck Vaughn, 1999.

Hyde, Margaret O. *Alcohol 101: An Overview for Teens*. Brookfield, CT: Twenty-First Century Books, 1999.

Johnson, Julie. *Why Do People Drink Alcohol?* Austin, TX: Raintree/Steck Vaughn, 2001.

Peacock, Nancy B. *Alcohol*. Philadelphia: Chelsea House, 2000.

Pringle, Laurence. *Drinking: A Risky Business*. New York: William Morrow, 2000.

Stewart, Gail B. *Teen Alcoholics*. San Diego: Lucent Books, 2000.

Organizations and Online Sites

Al-Anon Family Group Headquarters
http://www.al-anon.alateen.org
This online site offers helpful information for the families and friends of alcoholics.

Alcoholics Anonymous (AA)
http://www.alcoholics-anonymous.org
This online site provides information on one of the world's best known treatment choices for alcoholism.

Mothers Against Drunk Driving (MADD)
P.O. Box 541688
Dallas, TX 75354-1688

http://www.madd.org
This group strives to stop drunk driving.

National Clearinghouse for Alcohol and Drug Information
(NCADI)
P.O. Box 2345
Rockville, MD 20847-2345
http://www.health.org
This agency provides information on alcohol abuse as well as
referrals to treatment resources.

National Council on Alcoholism and Drug Dependence
(NCADD)
20 Exchange Place, Suite 2902
New York, NY 10005
http://www.ncadd.org
This organization provides information on many different
aspects of problem drinking.

National Institute on Alcohol Abuse and Alcoholism
(NIAAA)
6000 Executive Boulevard
Wilco Building
Bethesda, MD 20892-7003
http://www.niaaa.nih.gov
This government agency sponsors research on the causes and
treatments for alcohol abuse and alcoholism.

SADD, Inc.
Students Against Drunk Driving
P.O. Box 800
Marlboro, MA 01752
http://www.saddonline.org
This organization is made up of students who have taken a stand against drinking and driving and are encouraging others to do the same.

A Note on Sources

My work on this book began by contacting the National Institute on Alcohol Abuse and Alcoholism (NIAAA)—the government agency that supports about 90 percent of the nation's research on alcohol use. The Institute's press releases provided the latest findings while their staff readily answered questions. Data from a number of the institute's publications proved extremely helpful as well. These included their Ninth Annual Special Report to the U.S. Congress on Alcohol and Health along with such NIAAA journals as *Alcohol, Research and Health*, and *Alcohol World*. The U.S. Department of Transportation was also extremely informative in answering questions about the effects of drinking on driving.

Books that proved useful in tracing the history of alcohol included *Straight Up On The Rocks: A Cultural History of American Drink* by William Grimes and *Drinking In America: A History* by Mark Edward Lender and James Kirby Martin.

The quotes, stories, and some statistics scattered throughout the book came from a number of books, newspapers, magazines, and Internet sources. Among these were *The New York Times*, *Adolescence*, *USA Today*, *People Weekly*, *U.S. News & World Report*, *The Tech* (MIT's student newspaper), *A Drinker's Life* by Pete Hamill, Alcoholics Anonymous—Flint AA Online ,and CNN Interactive's "The Health Story Page."

Both the organizations Alcoholics Anonymous (AA) and Mothers Against Drunk Driving (MADD) provided valuable information. Additional insight into the toll alcoholism takes was gleaned through conversations with a number of people who had struggled with this problem.

—Elaine Landau

Index

Numbers in *italics* indicate illustrations.

About the Author

Popular author Elaine Landau worked as a newspaper reporter, editor, and as a youth services librarian before becoming a full-time writer. She has written more than 150 nonfiction books for young people. Included in her many books for Franklin Watts are other Watts Library titles on disasters and space, such as *Maritime Disasters* and *Jupiter*. Ms. Landau, who has a bachelor's degree in English and journalism from New York University and a master's degree in library and information science from Pratt Institute, lives in Miami, Florida, with her husband and son.